ISBN 978-1-330-58365-4
PIBN 10028425

HOW TO REFORM OUR PRISON SYSTEM

As they are to-day, English prisons are not only manufactories of crime, but forcing-houses for professional criminals. The human, not to say humane, note is absent from them. Routine, a deadly, dull, stupid routine, based on no logical principle, and having no objective point whatever, reigns supreme. Three centuries ago Paolo Sarpi, who was directed by the Venetian Government to investigate and report upon the prisons of Venice, wrote: "The object of punishment should be the emendation, not the destruction of the criminal." These were wise words, but they do not appear to have borne much fruit in 300 years.

The time, accordingly, appears to be opportune for directing attention to the defects of the English prison system, not only as regards reformation, but in other details. That system simply tends to make what I may term the accidental criminal an habitual criminal, to case-harden the old offender. It is a system lacking throughout in sympathy, which attempts nothing, and apparently cares nothing, in regard to the improvement of character, or in reference to preparing the incarcerated man or woman for return to the world. It is solely and only concerned about the performance of the daily routine and the safe custody of the prisoners. Its tendency is to atrophy every human feeling and lofty aspiration, and to induce and accelerate a moral and mental degeneracy. Whether from a utilitarian, a moral, a philosophical or a common-sense standpoint, it must stand utterly condemned. That it is not so condemned is simply due to the fact that the public have no conception of it as it is, know nothing indeed of it, save what they have been told by writers who have had no experience of its effects, and who frequently assume that because it is English it is superior to the prison systems of Continental nations. I have attentively studied these systems, and have no hesitation in asserting that in every important feature the English prison system lags far behind them.

It is true that in Siberia, as in New Caledonia and Cayenne, the ill-conducted convict is more severely punished than he is at Portland or Dartmoor. On the other hand, in the French and Russian penal settlements, the well-conducted convict, the man who aspires to rise from his condition of moral degradation, has opportunities and possibilities. In this country the man sentenced to penal servitude for life, even were he during his incarceration to be developed into a saintly character, is no better off, and in mental and bodily vigour is certainly much worse off, at the close of his incarceration than he was at the commencement. In Siberia his industry and good conduct would, when they had been sufficiently demonstrated, have obtained for him a condition of comparative freedom and comfort. And yet there are persons, well-meaning persons, in this country who can be indignant and wax eloquent concerning Siberian prison horrors, and the use of the knout in Siberian prisons. They have nothing to say, because they know nothing, about the dull, uninteresting and passive atrocities of Portland, Parkhurst and Dartmoor, and the cult of the lash there. These are English prisons, and, therefore, presumably beyond criticism. This manner of looking at vital questions is largely prevalent in this country. It has led to many false conclusions, and, not unnaturally I think, obtained for Great Britain on the part of Continental nations a reputation for hypocrisy, which is, however, largely an unconscious hypocrisy.

If the English people knew the English prison system as I know it, I feel perfectly certain it would be doomed. It is, I repeat, useless for any purpose, deterrent or reformative. It is based on no principle. It is terribly expensive. It is responsible for a constant manufacture of professional criminals and lunatics. What useful purpose, then, does it serve? Why continue it? Why not approach the whole question of the treatment of criminals in at least a rational spirit? And in order to assist a calm consideration of this matter, I ask my readers to clear their minds of prejudices and preconceived ideas, to investigate the subject for themselves, to ponder over the question what the aim of imprisonment ought to be, and, having done so, to decide how far short our prison system at present falls of that aim, and the steps that should be taken to effect and enforce a radical alteration.

Quite evidently the only means of forming a correct idea as to what the English prison system really is, is to have been an inmate of an English prison. The man who has had that experience is in a position to arrive at more correct conclusions in the matter than those persons, however good their intentions may be, who study those institutions altogether from the outside. Unfortunately, by far the greater number of those who have undergone incarceration in gaol are not educationally qualified to express their opinions in regard thereto. Of the comparative few who are so qualified many, if not most, desire only to forget the horrible past, and, if they have to look back on it, to regard it merely as a bad dream. Men shrink, naturally enough, from the notoriety in which any publication of their impressions of, or opinions respecting, prison life must necessarily involve them. And hence the public knowledge respecting the internal economy of British prisons is imperfect and, so far as my experience goes, highly inaccurate. The public conscience in the matter is, in fact, lulled. I want, if I can, to rouse it, and the best means to that end is to let the public see things as they are, and not as they are represented to be.

Now, I possess one qualification, at any rate, to write upon this subject. I have been an inmate of an English convict prison, and, as such, have had opportunities for studying in a practical manner one of those institutions which are recommended by some writers for the praiseworthy purposes of evolving "the enemies of Society into spiritual heroes," and of developing "manhood and self-reliance" in that somewhat large number of the population which, owing to bad education or unhealthy environment, is mentally and morally unsound. The fact of having been an inmate of one of these establishments is, I know full well, nothing to boast of; but, as I have said, unhappy as is the experience, it is, after all, an experience; and I propose to utilise it to correct erroneous opinions, and to convince my readers that inhuman remedies only aggravate and accentuate the evils which every one desires to see put an end to.

I am perfectly cognisant of the fact that, in a world which is admittedly imperfect, criticism of any institution or organisation or system is easy. The picking out of defects in anything or anybody is simplicity itself, and it is for some persons an extremely fascinating pursuit. I admit it is sometimes necessary to point out evils or defects in systems as in individuals, but the process should not be the mere outcome of a desire for captious criticism. I have never, in commenting on prison administration, confined myself to purely destructive criticism. To point out an evil is often not only necessary but incumbent; but, as a rule, the person who points it out should simultaneously suggest a remedy. And, accordingly, in this article I purpose setting forward the reforms in the English prison system which are in my opinion essential, if that system is to be rendered not only a humane one, worthy of a professedly civilised country, but necessary if the system is to provide for what, as the King has so well said, is "a matter of even more importance than punishment"—viz., the reformation of the criminal.

It is, I know, difficult, very difficult, to arouse interest, not to say enthusiasm, in regard to this matter of prison reform on the part of the great mass of the public. A large number of persons have a short, and to them satisfactory way of settling this question. They tersely sum up prisoners as "scoundrels" (with an adjective prefixed) for whom nothing is too bad, and they deprecate any attempt to improve their lot or to "molly-coddle" them, as these imperfectly-informed and quick-in-their-judgment people term it. There is another class, to whom I have already briefly alluded, who are strongly imbued with the idea, the outcome of patriotism run riot, that all English institutions are perfect, and that English prisons and the system administered therein, exemplify this national characteristic. And there is yet a third class which is simply ignorant and often apathetic. The object of this article is at one and the same time to attempt to convince and convert these three classes—a Herculean task I am aware, but not, therefore, necessarily hopeless.

A pithy aphorism of Carlyle occurs to me as singularly appropriate for the first class I have referred to. "Many a man thinks that it is goodness which keeps him from crime, when it is only his full stomach. On half allowance he would be as ugly and knavish as anybody. Don't mistake potatoes for principles." Ruskin must have had the third class in view when he wrote: "The plea of ignorance will never take away our responsibilities. It is written, 'If thou sayest, Behold, we knew it not; doth not He that pondereth the heart consider it? and He that keepeth thy soul, doth not He know it?'" As regards the second class, the self-complacent Englishman, the only way to rouse him is, I think, to shock him by flinging cold, hard facts at him.

My readers may take it from me that English prisons will never be reformative or educative or otherwise than they are at present, so long as they are under the Prison Commission—the most retrograde public body in this country. It cherishes and hugs all the evil traditions and ideas and feelings and prejudices of all the ex-prison governors of the past who have been members of it. Its only aspirations are to keep the prisoner securely in custody, to obviate any scandals in prison administration, and to prevent anything leaking out respecting the internal economy of English prisons, except through the mouths or pens of prison officials or ex-prison officials. And hence, when a chance visitor to one of His Majesty's prisons who has gone over it in the company of a prison official gives the impression of his half-hour's perambulation to the world, he depicts a veritable Arcadia wherein only man—the prisoner—is vile, while the officials are guardian angels who devote their lives to the ne'er-do-wells, scallywags, and off-scourings of society. On the other hand, when an ex-prisoner writes his impressions of prison life, his statements are discounted by officialdom. I have heard it asserted that all prisoners are liars, and that prison life tends to develop a fondness for deceit and untruthfulness.

The persons who so argue, for their own purposes, with great lack of humour fail to see that this statement is, in itself, a severe condemnation of the existing system, because it amounts to this, that the most civilised nation on the globe is not capable of evolving a better prison system than that which infallibly develops lying and deceit in prisoners. As I have remarked in many previous articles I have written respecting prison life, I have found prisoners just as other men. There are liars in prison as out of it. Truth is neither a prerogative nor a characteristic of any particular class. One thing may, however, be said. The ex-prisoner has no personal interest in concealing or perverting the truth about prison administration, while the prison official has. I am very strongly of opinion that were the Prison Commission abolished, and English prisons placed directly under the Home Secretary, the initial step would have been taken towards the reformation of those establishments. The Prison Commission has its antiquated ideas and deep-rooted prejudices, and it blocks the way of every reform. Even those reforms which have been forced upon it, it has rendered absolutely nugatory. Some nine years ago during the discussion of the Prisons Act of 1898, which, owing to the obstruction of the Prison Commission and prison officials has effected next to nothing, Sir Matthew White Ridley, the then Home Secretary, expressed himself shocked when he heard in the House of Commons that a man sentenced, perhaps, to penal servitude for life was not permitted to touch his wife's hand on the occasion of the brief visits she was permitted to pay him at long intervals. He promised that an alteration of this matter, as well as in regard to talking and other reforms —more light, lectures, etc.—should be effected. The Home Secretary's intentions were good, but he underestimated the resistance he would have to encounter from Prison Commissioners and prison officials "in the interests of discipline," that stereotyped formula which embodies the prejudices and fossilised ideas held by these persons on the subject of prison administration. The first essential reform, I repeat, in prison administration, is to make a clean sweep of the Prison Commission and bring the prisons directly under the Home Secretary, assisted by an Inspector-General, for which office a prison official should be absolutely disqualified.

And next in order of prison reforms I place the matter of diet, not because I deem it more important than some others—far from it—but because it is one which can be effected at once. Any person who has had the misfortune to have been in gaol, more especially in a convict prison, is painfully aware of the fact that food is a perennial topic of conversation, a fruitful source of complaint and discontent; and it is scarcely to be wondered at. After all, man is an animal, and requires a certain amount of food daily to nourish his frame and repair the waste of tissue. This quantity is a varying one, depending on many factors. Some men, it is well known, require much more food than others. The Prison Commissioners, however, decline to recognise this generally admitted fact. They have drawn up a scale of dietary sufficient, and not more than sufficient, for the average man, *provided he gets it;* too much for a few men, and far too little for many men—probably most. I have advisedly said "provided he gets it," and this is a very large proviso. There are many persons in gaol interested in seeing that the prisoner does not get his allowance. Not to put too fine a point upon it, there is a considerable amount of roguery in reference to both the quantity and quality of the food provided for prisoners. There is an utter, or almost utter, lack of supervision over the persons responsible for ordering these supplies, and checking the quantity and quality supplied, while in the kitchen there is still further leakage or wastage. I could write a considerable amount on this head, but I think I have said sufficient.

It may be taken as an incontrovertible fact that the average prisoner in a convict prison does not receive his proper allowance of food, that the quality of it is bad, and the cooking execrable. The latter fact is hardly to be wondered at, seeing that the cooks are amateurs, and the prison official who is ironically termed the "Master Cook" is an amateur likewise. Prisoners, of course, are permitted to make complaints respecting both the quantity and quality of their food, but this is a privilege which it is best not to exercise. According to the rules hung on the wall of each prisoner's cell, frivolous complaints respecting food are a breach of prison discipline, and will be punished as such. On only one occasion did I venture to complain of the quantity of the food issued to me. It was in respect of my dinner on a Monday, consisting, *inter alia*, of 2 ounces of boiled bacon. As the quantity issued to me when weighed just turned the scale at ¾ ounce, I made a complaint to the Governor on the subject. He informed me that bacon was weighed, according to the regulations, *before*, not *after*, cooking, and that my ration thereof had lost 1¼ ounces in the process. I inquired what I was to do supposing it were all lost, but to this inquiry I was not vouchsafed a reply. A scale of dietary which is the same for every man is, I reiterate, an absurdity.

The country pays sufficient for prisoners' food, and quite a large number of persons are amassing considerable sums of money at the expense of wretched prisoners. They are, in fact, robbing the men they denounce as "scoundrels" If the country, for reasons which appear good to it, deprives certain of the inhabitants of their liberty, and subjects them to punishments in which starvation is not detailed, it has no right to starve them. And since these persons are prevented from looking after those who supply them with food and taking effectual steps to see that they get what the regulations allow them, the country ought most certainly to undertake the duty. At present that duty is utterly neglected, and the curtailing (I might use a stronger word) of prisoners' food by prison officials and prison contractors is looked on as a huge jest. Even when a prison official is clumsy enough to be discovered committing robbery in gaol—robbery of the helpless—he is never prosecuted. It is deemed a venial offence. In my opinion it is one of the most scandalous, and should be punished with the utmost rigour of the law.

The food question affects a man directly he arrives in gaol, and accordingly I have placed it first. Having got the man into gaol (I am, I may remark, dealing only with long sentences—sentences of penal servitude), what should be done with him? He ought, I suggest, to be put to remunerative labour for which he is suited, and some portion of his earnings should be credited to him. This practice, I understand, obtains in several Continental prison systems, and its merits are obvious. It impels habits of industry, and it would enable the hard-working prisoner to earn by his own labours when in gaol sufficient to pay for his maintenance, and sufficient also to give him a start on his return to the world. At present the ordinary penal servitude prisoner is evolved into a loafer. He earns nothing; he is not allowed to earn anything. He is taught to idle, and told not to hurry over his job, as there is difficulty in finding him another. I am perfectly certain that the value of my labours during the three years and nine months of my incarceration did not aggregate £5. I was not allowed to work for my maintenance or to work for myself. Of course, remunerative labour in convict and other prisons will be impossible until the absurd idea that prison labour must not compete with outside labour is effectively knocked on the head. Why should it not? Prison industries certainly ought not to unduly compete with outside industries, but a man in a Government establishment yclept a prison may as reasonably be made to work at remunerative employment as a man in another establishment, yclept a dockyard or arsenal. The whole idea is based on nothing better than the fetish of a catch phrase. Prisons will never be rendered reformative establishments until that idiotic catch phrase is got rid of. If my ideas were adopted, these establishments, instead of being, as at present, houses of idleness, would be hives of industry. Then, and only then, will the discharged prisoner problem be effectively solved.

Simultaneously with the training of the prisoner in habits of industry, I would train and build up his mental capacities and his moral character. This will never be done by those marvellous rhetorical exercitations—prison sermons—nor can it be effectually accomplished, although it can be greatly aided, by a much needed improvement in the prison library. Ethics should be inculcated in prison, and the prisoner taught, not by flinging pointless platitudes at his head from the pulpit, but by appeals to his reason, making plain to him what ethical conduct is and the manifest advantages thereof. I would make lectures a prominent feature of prison life—lectures in the evening. It is stupid to send prisoners to bed at 8 o'clock. And yet any proposal to alter this senseless rule, and any suggestion that from 7 to 9 p.m. or 8 to 10 p.m. prisoners should be employed in cultivating their minds and in the process of building up character, will, I know, occasion much perturbation, and, possibly, much bad language among prison officials. These personages imagine that prison regulations are, like the laws of the Medes and Persians, unalterable; they, none of them, comprehend that rules are, after all, only means to an end. If the reformation of prisoners can be effected or aided by prisoners remaining up till 10 p.m., or even till midnight, let it be done. Better that a few prison officials should be inconvenienced, and mayhap shocked, than that we should go on manufacturing professional criminals instead of attempting to stop the process.

Prisoners should be placed in possession of all permitted privileges on arriving in gaol, and be deprived of them, if necessary, for purposes of punishment. The present practice is indefensible. A man is sentenced to a long term of penal servitude; he is taken away from his family and his friends; and yet *this* is the time when obstacles are placed in the way of his seeing, writing to, or hearing from his relatives. He must wait three or four years before he obtains even moderate facilities for these purposes. Obviously the time when the ordinary man desires to see and communicate in writing with his friends is immediately after conviction. His private affairs, in consequence of his conviction, are usually in a chaotic condition, and those who were dependent on him are left in blank ignorance respecting those affairs. This is the period his countrymen, or rather the Prison Commissioners, select for cutting him off from everybody, and giving him opportunity for six months' introspection and retrospection in solitary, or, as these officials, who are sticklers for verbal precision, prefer to term it "separate" confinement. The whole of this procedure is cruel and barbarous, unworthy of a humane or civilised nation. To my knowledge it drives many men mad, and even when it does not induce lunacy, mentally affects a large proportion of those subjected to it. The absurd thing about it is that there is nothing to be said in its favour, and that only the crass official obstinacy of the Prison Commission is responsible for its retention.

The cruel and degrading treatment of prisoners' relatives or friends when visiting them constitutes a grave scandal. A prisoner's wife or daughter, or other relation or friend, can only converse with him through a wire grating in the presence of a warder who walks up and down in a space between, while the visitor and visited have to shout at one another. And this in the twentieth century! No such brutal or torturing degradation exists in any Continental prison system. Its effect is to dehumanise men, and cut them off from healthy influences. The prisoner who has any respect for his relatives, and especially his female relatives, will not subject them to the degradation involved in such visits, while the time-limit—half an hour once in three or four months—is preposterous in the extreme. Just fancy the condition of mind of the wife who makes a journey from, say, the North of England to Portland or Dartmoor to see her husband under such conditions! Greater freedom should be permitted as regards letters and visits. The less a prisoner is thrown in on himself, and the more he is encouraged to foster his home ties, the less likely is he to descend into that condition of despair and demoralisation which are such potent factors in driving men to perdition.

Next, perhaps, to food, the restrictions, or attempted restrictions, on talking give rise to most of the discontent which from time to time breaks out in overt acts in prison. The theory of the Prison Commissioners is that even if a man be sentenced to penal servitude for life, and walk or sit day after day alongside a fellow-prisoner, he should never utter even such a remark as "Good morning," save on Sunday afternoons, when, after three years of imprisonment, if his conduct be good, he is allowed to walk in association, and converse with another prisoner for half an hour or so. Of course, this counsel of perfection of the Prison Commissioners is not observed. As a matter of fact, no prisoner observes it. How could he? The golden gift of silence upon which Carlyle dilated is given to but few men, and to be silent for twenty years save once a week is a little too much perfection to expect of human nature. And, accordingly, talking is always going on in convict prisons, and prisoners—some prisoners—are always being punished for talking. The Governor of a prison knows that every prisoner talks, the prison officials know it, for they hear it, and yet every day some half-dozen men are reported and punished for this heinous offence. The Governor listens quite seriously to the charge, quite seriously asks the prisoner what he has to say in his defence, and when the prisoner replies "Nothing," or that he talked just because everybody else talks, the Governor quite seriously sentences the prisoner to deprivation of remission marks, or to a course of bread and water. What arrant hypocrisy! Every one, including the Governor, knows full well that the man was "run in" merely because the reporting warder had a grudge against him, or considered, as all prison warders do, that it was necessary to keep himself *en evidence* by reporting somebody. If talking—talking out of working hours—were legalised, the discipline of His Majesty's prisons would be vastly improved. The merit—if it be a merit—of the talking restriction is that it places a weapon in the hand of prison officials to pay off a grudge against a prisoner. If talking in prison were sanctioned, it would in my opinion largely diminish in volume. As it is every prisoner feels himself impelled or compelled to talk, either as a protest against an absurd regulation, or so as not to appear to be something his fellow-prisoners are not.

Governors of prisons are always complaining that the establishments under their charge are under-staffed. Probably they are—as the system is administered. It may safely be asserted that English prisons are the most expensive in the world, and that there are proportionately more officials in them than in the prisons of any other country, civilised or uncivilised. This fact is due to another fact, that the prisoner, whatever his qualifications, ability, or conduct, is deemed and declared disqualified to hold any responsible position. He is, indeed, usually, on the "how-not-to-do-it" principle, which is so largely in evidence in His Majesty's prisons, put to work for which he is absolutely unfitted. Such an idiotic plan does not prevail in the prison systems of other nations. In them the services of a prisoner are utilised to the best possible advantage, and he is encouraged to rise to a position of trust. If this principle were recognised and adopted in this country, half of the prison officials might be got rid of, and the expense of prisons materially reduced. Even in the transportation days men were encouraged to rise, and did rise, from their dead selves to higher things. In Great Britain to-day a man sentenced to penal servitude for ten, fifteen, twenty years, or life, can rise to nothing. He is watched, hunted, supervised, from the day of his arrival in prison until his departure, if he does depart. Should he die, he will have the satisfaction of thinking that a prison warder will accompany his corpse to see it underground, for fear, presumably, the body might arise from the coffin and cheat the prison officials at the finish. It is a punishable offence for a prisoner during working hours to get out of the sight of his "officer." Even when obeying the calls of nature he is in view. When in his cell asleep he is periodically viewed through the spy-hole. No man is exempt from this espionage, simply because no man is trusted, however much and long he may have demonstrated his reliability, and however good his conduct may be. The result, of course, is, and I believe is intended to be, to utterly destroy the man's self-respect. He degenerates into a hunted animal, deemed fit for nothing but to be kept under lock and key, put to useless and degrading labour, and absolutely forbidden to employ his particular talents or abilities for himself or his country.

There are dozens—nay, hundreds—of reforms I might detail which are imperatively called for in the treatment of prisoners, but I have not space to deal with them. They would all naturally spring from the striking of the humane note, the adoption of an intelligent conception as to the object and purposes of prison. When these are in existence, we shall no longer grudge the prisoner God's light, and stint him in artificial light; we shall no longer crop close his hair, and array him in absurd garments designed to make him look villainous. We shall not, if he offends against discipline, punish him with "cat" or birch, because such treatment is inefficacious, cruel, degrading, and demoralising not only to the offender but to those who inflict it on him. We shall not be perpetually searching every prisoner and ransacking his cell, whether the man be good or bad, trustworthy or reliable. We shall, in a word, recognise that though this man is a prisoner he is still a human being, a stricken brother to be tended, whose moral wounds should be bound up and healed to prevent the poison therefrom spreading and infecting his whole system. At present these wounds are constantly being probed and irritated, with the consequence that the patient leaves prison in a putrid condition, a danger to himself and to others.

Yes, we want a new prison system; but we want also new men to administer it. The Scripture aphorism about the futility of putting new wine into old bottles is particularly appropriate here. The most perfect prison system yet devised or organised would fail, and would be bound to fail, were it attempted to be administered by the present staff. These men are saturated with the prejudices and ideas of the past, and imbued, most of them, with the notion that there is a natural enmity between them and the prisoner. For a new system there must be new men with new training, new conceptions of duty, higher ideas of responsibility. Furthermore, our prisons, both convict and local, should be more largely thrown open to the outside public. The visiting committee, which is now merely another name for the local magistrates, who are usually the registrars of the governor's decisions or advice, should be made popular bodies, whereon men and women who interest themselves in prisons and prisoners should be appointed. Prison inspectors, as they at present exist, are absolutely useless. They are always ex-prison governors, and are invariably on the side of officialdom. Such men never take any independent line, they regard prisoners' complaints with suspicion, and the words of one or half a dozen prisoners are of no avail against the word of one prison warder, however personally interested the latter may be in telling a falsehood.

And now a few words on another matter intimately connected with prison reform—the suggestion put forward by well-intentioned, but wrong-headed and ill-informed persons respecting the best means of dealing with professional crime. The desire to stamp out crime, and to put an end to the professional criminal class, whose existence is surely the grossest satire on our vaunted civilisation, will never be effected by shutting up a certain number of criminals in perpetuity. If we want to deal with any evil, it is essential, I think, to endeavour to ascertain the causes which produce or accentuate that evil, and, having discovered them, to seek to remove them simultaneously, or, prior to attempting, to cope with the evil itself. This is precisely what so many writers on the subject will not do. They persist in putting the cart before the horse. They assume that there is something fascinating, exhilarating, exciting in crime, and that the professional criminal is in very much the same condition as the confirmed drunkard—he cannot help himself, and, accordingly, should, like the drunkard, be placed under restraint, and kept under restraint, and trained to useful pursuits, which, however, he is not to be allowed to pursue save under detention and supervision. This is, it seems to me, a counsel of despair. Men are not so bad as these writers would have us believe. The criminal classes are not such hardened, hopeless, degraded beings as they suggest. Crime is, I contend, a disease, and ought to be treated as such. When an attack of typhoid fever is prevalent, simultaneously with the treatment of the patients, the drains in the neighbourhood of their houses are overhauled with a view to remedying the causes which led to the outbreak of the disease. The moral doctors in our midst decline, however, to follow the excellent example of their medical confrères. They are for giving the patient continual and nauseous doses of absolutely useless medicine. They suggest he should be regarded and maintained as a perpetual invalid, to be locked up for fear any germs of the disease should linger in his system, and be spread by him; but they obstinately refuse to attempt to build up the patient's system while under confinement, to subject it to healthy conditions, and at the same time to seek out and remove the insanitary causes that have occasioned or aggravated the disease. They will not do this because their diagnosis is faulty, and, accordingly, their medicine is absolutely noxious, and their suggestions futile.

The assumption that the professional criminal loves his profession and won't be quit of it, whatever opportunities are proffered him of earning an honest living, is not only not correct, but is egregiously false. Despite the assertions of many writers to the contrary, pocket-picking, burglary, and house-breaking, are not precisely the pursuits after which men hanker. How, then, it may be asked, comes it that so many criminals to whom a helping hand is held out on their release from gaol, return to wallow in the mire? The explanation seems to me to be simplicity itself. The charitable people, or pseudo-charitable people, are largely the cause of it. They make the path of the ex-criminal so hard, the building up of the character process so difficult. They want to reform the criminal in their own way, and that way is, I fear, an impossible one. It involves the patronising of the criminal, the impressing on him the fact that he is not as other men, constant supervision of and interference with him, putting him to uncongenial and ill-paid work, and making inquisitorial investigations in regard to the spending of the miserable pittance he receives.

The ex-prisoner is, in fact, regarded as a "one-legged" man, to be paid accordingly, and to be deemed a cripple, whose peregrinations must be carefully supervised for fear of his falling. He is not even to be allowed a wooden leg to get about on, but is to be led by the charitable organiser or the missionary until at last the moral cripple gets into a condition of desperation, curses charity and all its ways and instruments, remarks "better a thousand times to be in gaol," and returns, to use the hackneyed simile of these charitable people, to wallow in the mire. He missed the excitement of the criminal life, they tell us. Not so, good sirs. He was sick unto death of your patronage, your prying, your fussy interference, your plethora of Christian texts, and your utter lack of Christian charity. You are the real manufacturers of criminals, and until you change your methods and manners, and bring to bear on your efforts love and sympathy and fellow-feeling, whatever your motives, your results will be futile. You will merely accentuate the evil you profess a desire to remedy.

I believe in my heart that no man is a criminal from choice; at any rate, I have never come across one, and I have talked the matter over with many hundreds.

When a man has once come under the ban of the law in this country, the difficulty really is to avoid becoming one of the criminal classes. The way to that end is smooth; society has rendered, and still renders it so. "The world," to use that convenient abstraction, expects that a man who has been in gaol will continue on an evil course. It shuns him on his release, and will have nothing to say to him. If he makes an honest living, he can only, as a rule, do so by dint of hiding his past and changing his name. When his identity is discovered, and it usually is, he gets short shift, and has to commence again the effort to live under false pretences. He has the necessity of deceit borne in on him from the day of his release. His friends, if he have any, suggest it. Frequently, if not mostly, he finds the struggle a hopeless one, and if he succumb, and he often does succumb, it can at least be said, though we cannot pronounce him a hero, that society must share with him the responsibility of his fall. This is the way the criminal classes in this country are perpetually being recruited, and one of the first steps to put a stop to the constant acceleration to their ranks is to bring about a change in the treatment of the prisoner when in gaol, and in the attitude of society to him when he is released. To this end there is no need for any more charitable organisations. Charity should be an individual duty, to be individually performed. Charitable Societies are merely salves for the public conscience. It is an easy thing for a rich man to write a cheque for £100, and imagine that by sending it to some society he has discharged his duty to his neighbour. Often his money is wasted. One tithe of the amount spent, backed up by the individual effort of the drawer of the cheque, might have prevented one human being returning to the slough of crime.

In regard to the suggestions from time to time put forward to perpetually imprison what are called habitual criminals, who, during their life-long incarceration, are to be subjected to an educational and reformatory process, I cannot trust myself to express an opinion. Those who put forward such suggestions evidently know nothing of English prisons as they are. Men who make such proposals have a poor faith in humanity, a scant conception as to the meaning of human brotherhood and the duties it involves. I call no man altogether bad, incorrigible, or absolutely hopeless. No one deplores more than I do the existence of a distinct criminal class, but I say that society has created it, and continues daily to recruit it. Society must apply the remedy, and it lies ready at hand. Society, if the proposals of some writers on the subject were adopted, would take these human wrecks, permanently lock them up, and then, when the breath was out of their bodies, instruct the prison chaplain to read over their carcasses the sublime words of the Church of England Burial Service respecting "this our brother." "This our brother" Yes, but why wait till he is dead to proclaim this human tie? While there is life there is hope. If society would only regard the prisoner as "this our brother" during his life, and treat him as such, both in prison and on his release from prison, it would have gone far to solve one terrible social problem; for the criminal, assured that he was not a pariah of mankind, but a brother, stricken and soiled, to be tended and cheered and bid take heart and sin no more, would, I believe, become sensible of his ties and of his human treatment, and determine that he, too, would recognise his human kinship, its duties, its responsibilities.

CPSIA information can be obtained
at www.ICGtesting.com
Printed in the USA
BVOW06s1000080317
478101BV00014B/127/P

9 781330 583654